Clusters

A pronunciation practice book

Colin Mortimer

Drawings by Daria Gan

Cambridge University Press
Cambridge
London · New York · Melbourne

Published by the Syndics of the Cambridge University Press
The Pitt Building, Trumpington Street, Cambridge CB2 1RP
Bentley House, 200 Euston Road, London NW1 2DB
32 East 57th Street, New York, NY 10022, USA
296 Beaconsfield Parade, Middle Park, Melbourne 3206, Australia

First published 1977

Printed in Great Britain at the
University Press, Cambridge

ISBN 0 521 21625 7

Contents

Section Four: VCCC

Introduction

This practice book aims to help students who can pronounce individual English consonants, as in *s*at, *c*at or *r*at, but experience difficulty when these occur in clusters, as in *scr*eam, and even greater difficulty when words containing clusters occur in connected speech. It consists of fifty dialogues in which most of the clusters encountered in English are featured in context. Each dialogue concentrates on a specified cluster or group of clusters, indicated in phonemic transcription in the headings and in italics in the text. There are four sections:

Section 1

Two consonant clusters in word initial position, e.g. *sp*eak.

Section 2

Three consonant clusters in word initial position, e.g. *str*ong.

Section 3

Two consonant clusters in word final position, e.g. loo*ks*.

Section 4

Three consonant clusters in word final position, e.g. ga*sps*.

Revision dialogues are included in each section.

Using the book

There are many ways of using the dialogues, and variety is important. But in general it is suggested that before students practise a dialogue themselves they should first hear it spoken by a good model or models, to get a sense of the meaning and pronunciation of the whole. Then, individual words containing a featured cluster can be taken from the text and practised intensively. The next important step is to practise connecting these words with adjacent words in the text. Standard works on phonetics will provide descriptions of what happens at particular 'junctures' – e.g. when 'dra*gged*' is followed by 'down' in Dialogue 23. *It must be emphasised, however, that the chief aid here, as throughout, is a reliable model.* When clusters have been drilled in isolated words and in short combinations of words, students can work up to a fluent performance of the full dialogue – in chorus, groups and pairs if working in a class. Dialogues should be revised constantly, and some may usefully be memorised. The dialogues can be used as a basis for oral comprehension or oral composition, enabling students to practise maintaining pronunciation improvements while being to some extent 'distracted' by a consideration of meaning.

The recording

The dialogues are recorded on cassette, and all except the revision dialogues are preceded by a short *listen and repeat* section. In this section individual words containing featured clusters are spoken, with gaps for student repetition. The dialogues themselves are, of course, recorded without gaps, but teachers with a class, or students working individually, can use the pause and rewind mechanisms of their machines to play and repeat sections on which they may wish to concentrate.

Paced reading: Students often find it helpful to read *along with* the tape; to do this kind of paced reading it may be advisable to turn down the volume of the tape a little.

Phonetic symbols used in the text

p	*as in*	**pen** /pen/		s	*as in*	**so** /səʊ/
b	*as in*	**bad** /bæd/		z	*as in*	**zoo** /zu/
t	*as in*	**tea** /ti/		ʃ	*as in*	**she** /ʃi/
d	*as in*	**did** /dɪd/		ʒ	*as in*	**vision** /ˈvɪʒn/
k	*as in*	**cat** /kæt/		h	*as in*	**how** /haʊ/
g	*as in*	**get** /get/		m	*as in*	**man** /mæn/
tʃ	*as in*	**chin** /tʃɪn/		n	*as in*	**no** /nəʊ/
dʒ	*as in*	**June** /dʒun/		ŋ	*as in*	**sing** /sɪŋ/
f	*as in*	**fell** /fel/		l	*as in*	**leg** /leg/
v	*as in*	**voice** /vɔɪs/		r	*as in*	**red** /red/
θ	*as in*	**thin** /θɪn/		j	*as in*	**yes**/jes/
ð	*as in*	**then** /ðen/		w	*as in*	**wet** /wet/

6

Section One: CCV

1 pl bl pr br

A   *Please* go, *Brian.*

B   I *bring* you a beautiful *present,* and you tell me to **go**!

A   *Brian,* I ap*pre*ciate the *present,* but...

B   Would you *pre*fer a ***black*** * one?

A   *Brown* suits me perfectly, but...

B   Or a *blue* one?

A   But if your ***brother*** finds you here...

B   My *brother*? But surely *Brett's* gone to...

A   *Probably* that's him now.

B   *Blast*! *Blast*!

A   Oh. Perhaps it's only the *bread* man.

B   Good.

A   No. No, it **is** *Brett. Brett,* darling...

B   *Brett,* you *probably* won't **believe** this, but, er...

* Words in bold type should be given extra emphasis.

7

2 tr dr tw

A How are you *tr*avelling, *Tr*evor?
B By *tr*ain. The *tw*elve *tw*enty.
A Shall I *dr*ive you to the station?
B In all this *dr*eadful *tr*affic? Oh, no – I'll *tr*y to get a taxi.
A It's no *tr*ouble. Of course, if you don't *tr*ust my *dr*iving...
B Oh, I *tr*ust your ***dr*iving**, all right.
A Fine. *Tw*elve at your flat, then?
B Thanks. But *Tr*icia, the *tr*ip really is ***tr*emendously** important and...
A Mm?
B Well, the *tr*ain really **does** leave at *tw*elve *tw*enty.

3 kl gl kr gr kw

A You're back *qu*ickly. Didn't you go to the *cr*icket *cl*ub?
B Yes, I went.
A Was it *cr*owded?
B *Qu*ite *cr*owded.
A Was *Gr*eg there?
B *Gr*eg was there, yes. And *Qu*entin.
A But surely *Qu*entin **hates** *cr*icket.
B That's why they had a slight disagreement today.
A They *qu*arrelled?
B *Gr*eg threw a *gl*ass of beer at *Qu*entin.
A Oh dear.
B He missed, however.
A Mm. Shall I take your *cl*othes to the *cl*eaners?

4   fl fr

A   *Flatter* me, *Fr*ed.
B   *Flatter* you, *Fl*orrie?
A   *Fr*ank *fl*atters me, *Fr*ed.
B   *Fr*ank *fl*atters everybody.
A   He says I create a *fl*ame in his heart!
B   A *fl*ame in his heart?
A   A furious *fl*ame! He says I drive him **frantic**!
B   You drive me *fr*antic too, *Fl*orrie.
A   Oh, *Fr*ed! You old *fl*atterer!
B   *Fr*y the fish, *Fl*orrie.

5   θr

A   Only *three*pence?
B   Only *three*pence a *thr*ill.
A   I'll have *three*, please.

6 sp st sk

A   Ladies and gentlemen...
B   *Sp*eak up, *St*anley!
A   I *st*and before you...
B   *Sp*eak up, *St*anley!
A   On this *Sch*ool *Sp*eech Day...
B   Do *sp*eak **up**!
A   ON THIS *SCHOOL SPEECH* DAY...
B   *St*op **shouting**, *St*anley!
A   And I *sp*eak for both my wife and myself, when I say...
B   *Sp*eak up, *St*anley!
A   *SP*EAK UP *ST*ANLEY!!

7 sm sn sl sw

A   Is *Sn*owy at home? *Sn*owy *Sm*ith?
B   He's *sl*eeping. Go away.
A   *Sl*eeping? Where?
B   In there. Why do you *sm*ile?
A   Perhaps *Sn*owy is in there. But he isn't asleep.
B   I swear he's *sl*eeping.
A   When *Sn*owy sleeps, *Sn*owy *sn*ores. And when he *sn*ores, he **sn**ores! Hey, *Sn*owy! *Sn*owy! *Sn*owy, it's *Sl*im!
B   You see – no *sn*oring, *Sl*im.
A   It's the first time. Hey, *Sn*owy!
B   Doesn't he look *sw*eet?
A   *Sn*owy! Wake up! Wake up, *Sn*owy! *SN*OWY!
B   And now there's one *sl*ight *sn*ag.
A   A *sn*ag?
B   The *sm*all problem of what to do with **you**, *Sl*im.

8 ʃr

A   I shall *shr*iek!
B   *Shr*iek?
A   *Shr*iek!
B   Why *shr*iek?
A   *Shr*iek with terror!
B   They're only *shr*imps. A *shr*imp isn't anything to *shr*iek about. If there were a **shark**, of course...
A   Oh!!
B   Ah, well, *shr*impies – back into the water.
A   Good.
B   What **else** is there for tea?

9 Revise Dialogues 1–8

A This *plain black*? Or this *pretty brown*, perhaps?

B Can I *try that dress* on?

A This? It's *twice* as **expensive**, in fact. But I know you like **good** *cl*othes...

B It's **very** *gl*amorous.

A And it won't *crease*, of course.

B Mm. This shade of *green*'s *quite flattering* really.

A So *fresh*, isn't it? We had *three* of them, but two have been sold. Is it for a *special* occasion, by the way?

B The *St*aff Dance, at the *sch*ool, actually. Oh, dear – it's too *small*, Mrs *Sn*ell.

A Oh, dear! 1 must have been *sl*eeping! **I usually** ask!

B Don't worry. I'll find something else.

A No, no... What I mean is... Well, aren't Miss *Sw*ales and Miss *Shr*impton on your staff?

Section Two: CCCV

10 spl spr

A What a *spl*endid *Spr*ing day!
B A ***spl*endid** day!
A We'll *spr*ead our towels!
B *Spl*endid!
A We'll *spr*awl in the sun!
B *Spr*awl in the sun! *Spl*endid!
A We'll *spr*int along the beach!
B We'll ***spr*int**?
A **I'll** *spr*int.
B *Spl*endid!

11 str

A How *str*ong you are, Mr *Str*ong!
B All the *Str*ongs are *str*ong.
A But you're the *str*ongest!
B How *str*ange you are, Miss *Str*ange! I suppose all the *Str*anges are *str*ange.
A Yes?
B Ouch!
A And *str*ong!

12 skr skw

A   If you like noises
B   Noises in the night
A   *Squ*eaks, for example
B   *Squ*eals, for example
A   *Scr*atching and *scr*aping
B   *Squ*elching and *squ*awking
A   Then this is the place for you
B   And if you like *scr*eeches
A   *Scr*eeches and *scr*eams
B   Oh, if you like **screams**
A   You'll love it here
B   **Do** you like noises?

13 Revise Dialogues 10–12

A   *Str*oke it.
B   I'm not going to *str*oke it. It's *scr*uffy.
A   Only a **bit** *scr*uffy.
B   And it smells.
A   But not very *str*ongly.
B   **You** *str*oke it.
A   All right. Look. It likes me to *scr*atch its back.
      What a *spl*endid creature you are! Yes, you are!
      You're a *spl*endid...Oh! Ugh!!
B   Did it *squ*irt you?
A   *Squ*irt me? It *spl*ashed me! I'll **stink**!
B   But not very *str*ongly.
A   *Squ*alid creature!
B   Who? Me?
A   Ugh!

14 Revise Dialogues 1–12

A *Pl*ease, Mrs *Bl*ake, *pr*ess the *br*ake! Mind that *tr*ee!

B I've been *dr*iving for *tw*enty-nine years, young man.

A Careful! You **can't** *cl*ean your *gl*asses now! This is *cr*azy! Good *gr*ief!!

B *Qu*iet, *pl*ease. Why is he *fl*ashing his lights, d'you think?

A Sheer *fr*ight, *pr*obably! Foot off the **throttle**! Watch your *sp*eed! *St*op it! You'll *sk*id! Oh!!

B Only a *sm*all amount of *sn*ow on the road. Not *sl*ippery.

A Damn!

B No need to *sw*ear.

A Aargh!!

B Or *shr*iek. Ah, *spl*endid. Here you are. This is *Spr*att *Str*eet. As I say, *tw*enty-nine years, and never a *scr*atch.

A Thank you. Er...er, thank you. Goodbye. Goodbye.

B Take care *cr*ossing the *squ*are! The *tr*affic, you know!

Section Three: VCC

15 pt bd ps bz

A   We were ro*bbed*!
B   Stri*pped* of everything!
A   They jum*ped* out into the road...
B   And when we sto*pped*...
A   They gra*bbed* me and thum*ped* me in the ri*bs*...
B   And said if we didn't 'shut our tra*ps**'...
A   We'd be sta*bbed*.
B   They tied us with ro*pes*...
A   And dum*ped* us in the back of a van.
B   Finally they dro*pped* us at the bottom of these ste*ps*...
A   And the **polite** one I descri*bed* to you...
B   Oh, yes – **he** said he was sorry we'd been 'distur*bed*'!
A   And ho*ped* the ro*pes* weren't too tight!
B   Actually **he** was rather charming!

    * traps: mouths (slang).

16 ts dz

A   He just si*ts*.
B   That's all he does.
A   All day – si*ts* and si*ts*.
B   Occasionally he rea*ds*.
A   And ea*ts*.
B   But he ea*ts* very little.
A   We tell him he nee*ds* fresh air.
B   He nee*ds* frien*ds*.
A   He used to have lo*ts* of frien*ds*.
B   Loa*ds* of frien*ds*.
A   But now he just si*ts* and broo*ds*.
B   And he won't even **speak** to his ki*ds*.
A   He **still** says he has no regre*ts*, of course.
B   No regre*ts*. Mm.
A   Ah, well. What's the film at the Ri*tz*?

17 kt gd ks gz

A Who should we sele*ct*? Mr Di*cks*?
B Bra*gs* too much. Jo*kes* too much.
A Mr Bri*ggs*? Or Mr Fo*x*?
B Both ro*gues*.
A How about Mrs Wilco*x*?
B Na*gs* a lot. Who else is there?
A Only Miss Hi*ggs*.
B Too much intelle*ct*. Tal*ks* about boo*ks*.
A But she inspires respe*ct*. Anyway, you once told me you pi*cked* **me** for my intelle*ct*. And I've always na*gged*, you say.
B I pi*cked* **you** for your **loo*ks***.
A Miss Ton*ks* has nice **le*gs***. And when she ta*kes* off her **spe*cs***...
B Well?

17

18 tʃt dʒd

A We mar*ched* all day.

B We pi*tched* our ten*ts* by the river.

A Some of us sle*pt*. Some wa*tched*.

B In the morning, we bri*dged* the river.

A And mar*ched* again until we rea*ched* the battlefield.

B The battle ra*ged* for two nights.

A Some of us do*dged* the shells.

B Some of us mana*ged* to survive.

A The privile*ged* ones?

19 mp md mz

A Don't be alar*med* if she stamps

B Don't be alar*med* if she screa*ms*

A It's not what it see*ms*

B And if she calls you na*mes*

A Plays stupid ga*mes*

B Makes you ju*mp*

A Points at your hu*mp*

B Gives you bad drea*ms*

A Throws you in strea*ms*

B It's not what it see*ms*

A Don't be alar*med*

B You won't **really** be har*med*

20 nt nd

A He we*nt*. And he never retur*ned*.

B He we*nt* when?

A Oh, about the e*nd* of September.

B Well, I war*ned* you.

A Don't remi*nd* me.

B You ca*n't* say you were*n't* war*ned*.

A Anyway, he se*nt* the re*nt*.

B Have you fou*nd* a new tena*nt*?

A Yes – a frie*nd*. Peg Bo*nd*. There wo*n't* be any problems.

B I hope there wo*n't*.

A You do*n't* know Peg, of course?

B Well...I once le*nt* her a pou*nd*!

21   nθ ns nz

A   Bye, Flore*nce*. See you in a mo*nth*. Oh – if Vi*nce* pho*nes*...
B   Vi*nce* who?
A   Vi*nce* Bur*ns*.
B   Vi*nce* Bur*ns*? Not **the** Vi*nce* Bur*ns*?
A   Yes. If he pho*nes*, tell him...
B   You know Vi*nce* Bur*ns*?
A   Course. And if he pho*nes*...
B   I have a cha*nce* to talk to Vi*nce* Bur*ns*?
A   Say I'll be back on the te*nth*, probably...
B   'She'll be back on the te*nth*, Mr Bur*ns*....'
A   And if I'm not...
B   'And if she's not, Mr Bur*ns*, my name is Flore*nce*...

22   ntʃ ndʒ

A   Tomorrow we lau*nch* our new sales campaign. I'm giving a lu*nch*
     at our city bra*nch*. In the staff lou*nge*. Do come.
B   D'you know, Bla*nche*, your last lu*nch* added an i*nch* to my
     waistline.
A   I see no cha*nge*.
B   Look. I have a pau*nch*! I'm going on a diet!
A   Oh.
B   Immediately after your lu*nch*.

19

A   I po*pped* out to the sho*ps*, as I always do. And a man gra*bbed* my handbag.

B   Now, Mrs Ho*bbs*, le*t's* have a description of this man – in your own wor*ds*.

A   Well, I never loo*ked* at him properly – I was dra*gged* down, you know. But as I clu*tched* at his le*gs*...

B   Yes?

A   I saw his so*cks*!

B   Good.   Excellent.

A   They were exactly like my husba*nd*, Ja*mes*, wears.

B   Oh? And, er... what colour?

A   They were grey o*nes*. Plain grey.

B   Plain grey. I see, yes. Very useful.

A   But of course, **he** wouldn't pi*nch** my bag. Would he?

   * pinch: steal (slang).

24 ŋd ŋk ŋz

A They ba*nged* go*ngs*
B Sang so*ngs*
A Everyone dra*nk* the wine
B And as the sun sa*nk*
A The crowds thro*nged* to the river ba*nk*
B I thi*nk* of such thi*ngs* from time to time
A One lo*ngs* for them, occasionally

25 lp lt ld ltʃ ldʒ lk

A I bui*lt* her a palace. Dressed her in si*lk*.
   Her purse is fi*lled* with gold. She bathes in mi*lk*. Her caskets bu*lge* with treasure. And yet she will not yie*ld*. Why does she su*lk*?
B I cannot he*lp* it. How can I yie*ld* when he comes from the fie*ld* in boots that sque*lch*? And **must** he be*lch*?

26 lm lf lv lθ lz

A It was a good life, A*lf*.
B A fine life, Wi*lf*.
A Remember the ga*les*?
B And the wha*les*?
A And the sea*ls*?
B And the horrible mea*ls*?
A They should've made a fi*lm* about it!
B 'A*lf* and Wi*lf* at the He*lm*'!
A 'Life Aboard **The Reso*lve***'!
B Hm!
A Well, good hea*lth*!
B Cheers, Wi*lf*!
A Hey, d'you remember those what's-its-name gir*ls*?
B Mm. Preferred the mother, myse*lf*!

27   ft vd fθ fs vz

A He's not on the fourth floor now, he's been mo*ved* – to the fi*fth*.
   Use the li*ft*. I'll ring to say you've arri*ved*.
B No hurry. Er. . . how is he, Nurse?
A I think he's impro*ved*. Still cou*ghs* a lot, of course.
B And he beha*ves* all right, does he?
A Oh, yes. We have plenty of lau*ghs*! We'll miss him when he lea*ves*!
B He lo*ves* pretty nurses, Grandad does! It's a family weakness!
   By the way, he wanted me to bring him this gi*ft*. For his special
   favourite – a nurse called So*ft*.
A How lovely!
B Funny name, So*ft*, isn't it?
A Yes. But I've got u*sed* to it.
B Oh. Sorry.
A Well, I'll ring to say you've arri*ved*.
B I'm **sorry**!

28   θt ðd θs ðz

A Who ba*ths* you?
B **She** ba*ths* me. She's **always** ba*thed* me.
A Who clo*thes* you?
B **She** clo*thes* me. She's **always** clo*thed* me.
A And yet she loa*thes* you?
B She's **always** loa*thed* me!

A

1st JUNE
Ocean Hotel. Fir*st* class breakfa*st*.
   Toa*st* beautifully cri*sp*.
Went for a bri*sk* walk.
La*zed* by the pool.
Splendid lunch. Roa*st* chicken.
   Brai*sed* celery.
Ga*zed* at the sea. Do*zed* happily
   till du*sk*.
Dre*ssed* for dinner.
At dinner, met a mo*st* **charming**
   woman!

B

1st JUNE
Ocean Hotel. Breakfa*st* – the wor*st*
   ever!
Was stung by a wa*sp*.
Got lo*st*.
Having got lo*st*,
   mi*ssed* lunch.
Also,
   mi*ssed* the la*st* po*st*.
Tore my be*st* dress. Late for dinner.
At dinner, met a mo*st* **dreary**
   man!

* When read aloud, this dialogue is more effective if 'A' reads one line of his
  diary then 'B' one line of hers – and so on.

30 ʃt ʒd

A Face wa*shed*
B Nails poli*shed*
A Lips roug*ed*
B Off to her first ball
A Hopes da*shed*
B Spirits cru*shed*
A Dreams demoli*shed*
B Oh, well

31 Revise Dialogues 24–30

A We saw 'They Ha*nged* Fra*nk* Jenni*ngs*.'
B It was a **very** o*ld* film. I **loa*thed*** it. Wi*shed* I'd le*ft* after the fir*st* reel.
A I lo*ved* it. Better than those **modern** thi*ngs* – all viole*nce* and fi*lth*. I like a fi*lm* where virtue prevai*ls*.
B But surely **evil** prevai*led*! Fra*nk* was the **hero**! And they **ha*nged*** him!
A But his death **pro*ved*** something! Didn't you see the expression in the Sheri*ff's* eyes, just before the fi*lm* fini*shed*?
B I must've mi*ssed* that bit.

32 Revise Dialogues 15–30

A The ju*mp* we*nt* well. They didn't see our parachu*tes*, tha*nk* God! We rea*ched* the target area OK, and mana*ged* to surprise them. We destroyed **both** targe*ts*, and mo*ved* back before they reali*sed* what had happe*ned* – which was lucky, because they had more gu*ns* than we'd imagi*ned* – very well concea*led*, very well camouflag*ed*. It would've been bulle*ts*, she*lls*, mortar bo*mbs*, rocke*ts* – the lot! The helicopter pi*cked* us up as pla*nned* – and here we are, Sir. All prese*nt* and corre*ct*.
B Good. Ten minu*tes* later, and you'd have mi*ssed* lunch.

Section Four: VCCC

33 pts pst pθs

A My life has colla*psed*! My **world** has colla*psed*!
B Colla*psed*?
A Colla*psed*!
B I see.
A But if she ado*pts* me as her son, I shall be rescued from the **de*pths***!
B De*pths*? **What** de*pths*?
A The de*pths* of despair! The de*pths* of degradation! The de*pths* of...
B Poverty?
A Really, Maurice! How unworthy!
B And if she o*pts* to do otherwise?
A Back to the de*pths*! The de*pths* of humiliation! The de*pths* of dark, excruciating terror. The...
B Who writes your scri*pts*, by the way?

34 tθs–dθs* tst–dst*

A The wi*dths* are different!
B They're the same.
A They're entirely different!
B Identical. No difference at all in the wi*dths*.
A Look – here's a ruler! I'll measure them! See! The wi*dths* **are** different! Look!
B Nonsense. You are wrong. Gentlemen, it seems we have a trouble maker in our mi*dst*.
A But surely all of you can **see** that the wi*dths*...
B Take him away.

* Alternative pronunciations of 'widths' and 'midst'. Note, however, that 'eighths' has |tθs| only.

25

A   He's one of our most important conta*cts*. But difficult. How did you do it, Samantha?

B   Oh, he mi*xed* me a drink. We rela*xed*. And I coa*xed* him into agreeing to look at our produ*cts*. I've fi*xed* an appointment for the si*xth*. And if he rea*cts* favourably . . .

A   Excellent.

B   He's sweet, by the way – as I've always said.

A   Hm! That confli*cts* with **John's** view of him!

B   Well, John **always** contradi*cts* my opinions.

A   And, of course, you differ in certain **other** important respe*cts*!

36 mpt mps mft mfs

A His pro*mpt* action ultimately led to their arrest. Good triu*mphs* over evil in the end, you know, Mrs Smith – as I've always said.

B Mm. Of course, he got those **lu*mps*** on his head when they ju*mped* on him and du*mped* him down that well. And he still li*mps*.

A Yes, yes.

B Anyway, I'm glad to know that good triu*mphed* in the end.

A Indeed.

B What punishment will they get, by the way?

37 nts ndz

A Some men work with their mi*nds*

B Godfrey works with his ha*nds*

A But as his assista*nts*

B His age*nts*

A We handle the business arrangeme*nts*

B We know the requireme*nts* of the market

A How the trade wi*nds* blow

B Where to find suitable clie*nts*

A Appropriate distribution poi*nts*

B For the pou*nds* that Godfrey pri*nts*

38 nθs nst

A If only they could've waited! Even six mo*nths*!

B Or a couple of mo*nths*, anyway.

A We've nothing **against** him, of course.

B Nothing at all.

A They're so young and inexperie*nced*!

B Yes. But how experie*nced* were we?

A We courted for **years** before our engagement was annou*nced*!

B Years, dear?

A Well, if you're sure they'll be happy...

B I'm convi*nced*.

39 ntʃt ndʒd

A   'He lu*ng*ed at me with a knife. I pu*nch*ed him. He dropped it. He cri*ng*ed in the corner, teeth tightly cle*nch*ed, eyes filled with hatred. "I'll be reve*ng*ed!" he snarled. I pu*nch*ed him again. Harder...'

B   ...Then I lu*nch*ed with Jenny, as arra*ng*ed.

A   Oh, hello!

B   Nearly finished your chapter?

40 ŋkt ŋks

A   You see, as the exchange rate si*nks*, the value of your savings shri*nks*. But it you **ba*nk*ed** your money, instead of keeping it... wherever you keep it... it could earn **interest,** to some extent li*nk*ed to the cost of living.

B   No, tha*nks*.

A   Where **do** you keep it, by the way?

41 lpt lkt lps lts lks

A   She su*lks*.

B   She always **has** su*lk*ed.

A   And you should hear the insu*lts*!

B   She insu*lts* him all the time.

A   She never he*lps* him.

B   Never **has** he*lp*ed.

A   Well, we warned him.

B   Oh, we warned him.

A   We forecast the resu*lts*.

B   We did.

A   Finish your ice-cream, Harold – before it me*lts*.

42 lbz ldz ltʃt ldʒd

A These bu*lbs* were fi*lched** from Reynolds.

B You mean Reynolds, the wor*ld's* leading expert on daffodils, who ho*lds* the secret of the fabulous **blue** daffodil, which he has sworn will never be divu*lged*?

A No. Not that Reynolds.

* filched: stolen.

43 lmd lmz

A One of your most famous fi*lms* was about an enormous monster that overwhe*lms* a city. You played the monster, didn't you?

B That's right. It was fi*lmed* in the studio, of course. And the city I overwhe*lmed* was only a small, plaster-board model. Even so, I managed to break my **toe** in rehearsal!

A I'll never forget the bit where you kicked the Marine Hotel into the sea!

B With my **left** foot, you'd notice!

HOTEL MARINA

44 lfs lfθ lvd lvz

A If you look on the library she*lves*, you will find 'A History of the Rudo*lphs*'. The Rudo*lphs* were a large, rich, but **unlucky** family. They had thirteen children. The first eleven were invo*lved* in mysterious, fatal accidents. And the twe*lfth*, Randolph...Poor Rando*lph's* end was terrible. Eaten by wo*lves*, I'm afraid.

B And the remaining child? The last of the Rudo*lphs*?

A I was lucky. I inherited everything.

45 lθs lst

A I was alone. Missing you.

B So whi*lst* I was away, you opened my **last** bottle of champagne!

A I drank your health, darling!

B From **two** glasses?

A And **my** health, darling! I drank **both** our hea*lths*!

46 sps sts spt skt sks

A The hotel caters mainly for touri*sts*.

B As usual, they ga*sped* in terror as we whi*sked* away the bedclothes.

A And as we whi*sked* away the pillows, there were more ga*sps*...

B Even though these ta*sks* were performed nicely.

A None of the gue*sts* ever reque*sts* a second night in the haunted room.

B As ho*sts*...

A Resident gho*sts*...

B We find this so disappointing.

47 fts fθs

A We have now completed our customer survey, Sir. Of the total
numbers going up to the Arts and Cra*fts*, and Gi*fts* Departments,
three fi*fths* used the escalator, **two** fi*fths* used the li*fts*, and **one** fifth
used the steps, Sir.

B **Six** fi*fths*, Mr To*fts*?

48   Revise Dialogues 33–40

A   He's not the only experie*nced* observer here
B   Though he a*cts* as though he is
A   He's been warning us for mo*nths*
B   He insi*sts* that prompt action is vital
A   He wa*nts* us to move **out**
B   Into te*nts*
A   Well, if he thi*nks* we'll do **that**
B   He must think we're out of our **mi*nds***
A   Of course, we **have** heard a few noises
B   One or two sou*nds*
A   But we remain convi*nced*
B   Totally convi*nced*
A   That our volcano **never** eru*pts*

49   Revise Dialogues 41–47

A   I he*lped* him all I could!
B   You overwhe*lmed* him with kindness.
A   I gave him gi*fts*! Everything he a*sked* for!
B   You indu*lged* his every desire.
A   I was a fool to get invo*lved* with him! An absolute fool!
B   Even so, **shouting** never so*lves* anything.
A   WHAT D'YOU MEAN, 'EVEN SO'?

50   Conclusion

A   Now you've *practised* lo*ts* of *cl*usters.
B   Yes, but only with two and *three* consona*nts*.
B   All right, then – say 'Four *twelfths* make two si*xths*.'
B   Easy. Four twe*l*. . .